'More' by Matt Ward is a very good read. It's a different perspective on how to interact with people. This book is an incredibly useful tool for membership organizations in recruiting and retaining members of the association and individual chapter. As a Quality Professional, I consider this required reading for any group that wants to grow their membership! – John Conner, ASQ Regional Director

---

If you ever feel awkward in a business meeting setting, or if you dread networking events, this book will take your comfort zone to a higher level. Matt takes your hand and walks you through a human dynamic that is not taught in business school. You will be well-served to read this book. – Michelle Girasole, CEO, Fresh

---

The stronger your relationships with those who matter most to your business, the more resilient your business will be. In More, Matt Ward provides strategic insight and a directly applicable roadmap for building relationships that will serve your organization for decades to come. - Melissa Agnes, Crisis Management Advisor, Author, and Keynote Speaker

---

It is a book full of heart and full of practical steps that are easy to take, even if you are the opposite of a marketing genius like myself (despite my talkativeness, I am at heart very shy). So I recommend you give Matt Ward's book "MORE . . ." a read, if you want your contacts to have you top of mind because of a genuine relationship of caring that you have consciously cultivated with them. – Karen Bauer

If you're the kind of person who asks themselves each day "what's one thing I can do to get closer to my business goals?", the first thing you can do is buy this book, the second thing is open to any page and do that. Whatever is on that page, do that one thing that day and you'll be knocking out goals in no time. – Cailte Kelley, Financial Advisor

In a clear and concise tone, Matt Ward has laid out his pathway to MORE word of mouth referrals that lead to lifelong customers and sales success. In addition to being competent, trusted and responsive, Matt tells us to show our clients and prospects that we CARE. MORE provides a step-by-step plan to get the word out and make an impact that leads to referral relationships that last. Read MORE and get MORE! – Len Leader Vision Payroll

MORE is like having a conversation with an old friend. In this case, your old friend calls you to be the best version of your authentic and caring self, treating business contacts just as he treats you...like a friend. Offering tips for making the process easy, yet professional, MORE could well revolutionize the dynamics of business networking. – Laura Frombach, Sr. Product Manager, Lenovo

Matt creates a simple, easy to follow plan. What he says is second nature when making a friend and growing that friendship. Here he shows you how to use those actions and skills to build real connections in business. Intuitive and worth reading. – Marcia Maglione-Flynn, Communications & Special Projects Manager, Community Health Connections

Easily referenceable. I have never thought of some of those things really. – Frank Hynes, IT Professional 2

This book is a must read for every business owner and sales person looking to grow their business through referrals and networking the right way. – Frank Andreotti III MBA

If you're looking for more referrals from customers who love you this is a must-read. Matt Ward's CarePackage approach is a simple, easy to follow path for creating stronger relationships to grow your business. Love all the specific ideas for connecting with customers in creative ways--they will make you stand out and keep you top of mind when people are asked for referrals! – Michael Hudson, Speaker, Big Idea Guru LLC

As business owners we all understand the importance of building relationships. The challenge is to accomplish that without coming across as over selling. Matt Ward's book MORE, offers powerful tips that you can implement today to help you grow your business. I highly recommend that you read this book and send a copy to your best clients. It is one of the tips in the book. – Kevin Willett, Author, CEO New England B2B Networking Group

Great tips to stay current, remain memorable and build lasting business relationships. - Mark Bowden, author of best seller Truth & Lies: What People Are Really Thinking

More is a remarkable, easy-to-read and follow roadmap for how you too can make your clients think of you all the time. Not only does he tell you what to do, he gives you real examples of how to do it. I would add his book to the list of books to give to your clients in the chapter about "Brain Hacking with Books" (but he would never say that because he isn't in this for his own benefit)!!! This is a must-read book for anyone in sales. I will certainly be buying it for my clients. – Andrea Goodman, Owner, Swampdrainer

---

This is a terrific read that will engage you in Matt's world of creating and keeping quality clients. He offers doable, successful strategies that you will actually enjoy implementing and reading about. I highly recommend this for your business whether it's small or large! – Kathy Alexander, Vice President, J R Glass

---

Matt has expanded on a theme we can using reminding of. Kindness, manners and doing business with the 'right intent.' Easy read with doable, immediate, action steps! – Bambi Azarian, Realtor

---

In an age where we're inundated with technology and human interactions are becoming more brief and transactional, Matt Ward reminds us to slow down and focus on what matters most--people! Whether you consider yourself to be a master networker or you're so introverted that you hide from your own company, "More..." offers great tips for building deeper relationships based on delighting others. From the CarePackage pillars to making introductions and connections for the greater good, "More..." reminds us that we have innumerable tools at our disposal to be of service to others. The best part of Matt's strategies is that, when implemented, not only will readers enjoy making others genuinely happy, but they'll get referrals and new business too! It doesn't get any better. – Crystal Washington – Futurist, Technology Marketing Strategist, International Keynote Speaker

I love this new book by Matt Ward! Simple, common sense techniques to help me stay top of mind with current and past clients, and to systematically generate more referral business. As a realtor, over half of my business is from repeat clients or referrals, so this book is a game changer for me. Matt's book helps you to spontaneously show your love through thoughtful gifts and touches that are inexpensive but very powerful. I highly recommend this book for anyone who wants to significantly improve their repeat and referral business. – Luke Menkes, Realtor

MORE...

WORD OF MOUTH REFERRALS,
LIFELONG CUSTOMERS & RAVING FANS

MATT WARD

© 2018 by **Matt Ward**

Founders Hall Press

www.FoundersHallPress.com

www.Breakthrough-Champion.com

ISBN - 978-1-7326516-0-9 - eBook

ISBN - 978-1-7326516-1-6 - Paperback

Table of Contents

TO LISA

WITHOUT YOUR SUPPORT, THIS BOOK, AND THIS LIFE WOULD NOT BE WHAT IT IS. YOU EMPOWER ME EVERY DAY TO CHANGE THE WORLD. YOU ARE THE WIND IN MY SAILS AND THE FUEL IN MY ENGINE. THANK YOU FOR BEING YOU AND ALLOWING ME TO BE ME.

ACKNOWLEDGMENTS

There are countless individuals who have taught me many things in my life both personally and professionally. I could never thank all of you individually, but please know, I don't forget who you are, and what you have done for me.

To those of you that gave me a chance, who took a chance on me when I needed a job, who took a chance on me with an unproven web company early on, and those that stuck by us for all 16 years, I am eternally grateful. Without your trust, none of it would have been possible.

Mom – I have known for many years the sacrifices and difficult decisions you were faced with during the years I have been on this earth. I'm profoundly grateful that you are MY mom. Your resiliency has proven to be a very effective personality trait that you have taught me.

Milton Hershey –I never had the honor of meeting you in person, but you sir, have changed the course of my life for the better. Without your generous gift of Milton Hershey School, I don't know what my life would have been. While it's true that it is me that has done the work, it was you that gave me the opportunity to do that work and it was you that instilled the values that Milton Hershey School lives by today and continues to use to shape the lives of over 10,000 kids.

Dan Candell – My podcast co-host, you sir, are a real treat to have as a friend. I'm honored to have you in my life and know that I can call you at any time. Your ideas are fresh, your support is unwavering, and your friendship is immeasurable!

Jeff Cobb, Sonja Stetzler, and Gary Wilbers – You've become my sounding board. You encouraged me when I wasn't sure where to go with this book, and you've all supported me in a way I never thought a group of colleagues could.

Erik Wahl – 2011 was quite a few years ago, but to me, it still seems like yesterday. That day in Leominster Massachusetts, was the day you taught me about creativity, stepping outside the box, and doing things differently! It was also the day that set in motion, my career trajectory as a speaker. I'm honored that you've mentored me and provided insight into this industry. I'm honored to be the #ArtDropSniper and I'm thankful for all that I have learned from you.

Erica Milano – a simple five-minute conversation on a Pop Warner field in 2001, forever changed the course of my life! I'll never forget your idea, your words, and your encouragement. That conversation was the seed that turned into a profitable website agency, which I sold! Thank you!

FOREWORD

Think back to a time when someone sent you a gift in the mail, or just reached out to you for no other reason than to just let you know that they were thinking about you. It makes you feel good, doesn't it? Now, think back to a time when someone reached out to you, and you knew it was only because they wanted something… That's not a great feeling, is it? It's a human need to feel cared for, loved and acknowledged. However, those connections that we form with people must be genuine.

Matt Ward has a way to make sure his generosity, loyalty and giving nature is always genuine and altruistic. At first, I thought it's just Matt's nature, it's just his personality or one of his core values. Then I saw him mold a room full of dozens of business owners into truly caring beings, who upon leaving Matt's presentation, were all instilled with the values and principles that led Matt and every business that he has owned to be successful. It is an art, a skill and a trait of really and genuinely caring for others.

I first met Matt Ward at a local BNI group. There was something intriguing about his larger than life personality. As I went to more meetings and started to really study Matt (that's what I do, study human behavior…), I noticed that he had an amazing skill to make every single person in that group feel important. It didn't really hit me until Matt found out I was having trouble with a new laptop computer that I purchased. He offered to meet me for breakfast after the meeting and give me a crash course on how to work this newfangled laptop, as he had the same one. After several other interactions with him, we started to work on a few projects together. I must admit though, he had to twist my arm a little. After working in many failed business partnerships with others, I vowed to never work with someone again unless we both could contribute equally.

We started off developing a golf training program that we were selling to golf pros. It was moderately successful. After taking a break from that venture, Matt hit me with a curveball. He called me late one night and asked, "Dan, you have a great radio voice. Have you ever thought about going on the radio?" My ego got in the way and I said, "Matt, come on! You know I have been on the radio several times…" There, he introduced the idea to me of starting a joint venture podcast. It was rocky getting started, but now, nearly two years and almost 100 episodes in at the time I am writing this, it became a smashing success!

You may be wondering, why does all this matter? Over the course of sharing this podcast platform with Matt, going to several events with him, and forming a brotherly bond with him, I discovered something… He has such a unique way of caring for people. He listens, he observes and then he acts. What's amazing about this, though? He never expects anything in return. Does it help him and his business ventures? Absolutely! But it is his mindset about his giving nature that is truly remarkable.

I used to think that this was just a personality trait of Matt until I started asking him more about his values of genuinely caring. I was amazed that he started to instill the same values and principles in me, and then in others who have the pleasure of seeing him speak or who are in one of his programs. That's why I am elated that Matt wrote this book.

It sounds silly that nowadays people have to be taught values of caring and generosity, but it's true. These are values that seem to be slowly fading away amongst businesses and even individuals.

In this book, Matt has really cracked the code to a program that he will teach you called CarePackage. He teaches you how to apply these principles to your own life and business to create lifelong referral sources, customers and connections through the art of caring. Yes, it really is an art, and it is one that can easily be taught and applied to your life and to your business.

After being introduced to the content in this book, I was amazed at how simple yet effective this art is. Just to give you an idea, here is the first time I saw the power of CarePackage in action. I was speaking in Las Vegas to a group of 130 sales professionals. I was the last spot, the closing keynote. After my presentation, I decided to stick around to see how they closed out the event. It ended with the organizer of the event getting everyone to stand up and say one way that they were going to take action and implement what they had learned over the weekend of the conference. After each person stood up and gave an action item, the entire room chanted "I CAN, AND I WILL!" I didn't know it at the time, but this was the mantra of the group. I quickly jotted down the words, "I can, and I will" in my notebook. As I was about to leave, the co-organizer said, "Hey Dan, I love your notebook, where did you get it?" I smiled and said, "On Amazon!"

Upon leaving, I jotted down the key players in the organization, Sarah and Jim. Next to Sarah's name, I wrote down the words, "I can, and I will." Next to Jim's name, I wrote, "productivity journal." I put my journal away, flew home and went about my business.

About three weeks later, I was walking through a local department store and I walked by the section that had all of these wooden signs with sayings on them. I stopped, and one jumped out at me. I said, "Well, I'll be damned..." It had the words, "I can, and I will" written across the sign. It was $4.99. I immediately grabbed it and put it in my cart. That reminded me of what Jim had said about how he liked my journal. So, I went on my phone and ordered the same journal and had it shipped to Jim with a little note in it. As soon as I got home, I packed and shipped the sign to Sarah.

I was excited. I was more excited to wait to hear their responses... After a couple weeks of not hearing from them, I was a little disappointed. I called Matt and said, "DUDE! I did your thing, I cared! But they didn't care back, what the heck!" Matt reminded me, "that's not why we implement CarePackage. We do it to make others feel good, and we feel good because of that. We don't do it to get a response from them. We do it because we care." That was a big realization for me. But it's true.

A few weeks later, I ended up getting a note from both Sarah and Jim thanking me. I don't know if anything will ever come of that, I'm not expecting anything to come from it actually... I just know that little gesture of kindness and caring really put smiles on the faces of two people. And yes, it really is that easy.

Is there more to it than that? Absolutely. In this book, Matt will share his strategies, formula and special art of how to get more referrals and lifelong customers through CarePackage. This is a system that everyone can and should use. I can guarantee, even if you already apply similar principles, you'll still learn more strategies of how you can make these caring values even stronger.

Thank you for allowing me to share my experiences with you, and it really is a great pleasure knowing that more people will be applying this art to their network. As always, be well, do good, and be true to who you are.

Dan Candell

Board Certified Hypnotist & Speaker

INTRODUCTION TO CAREPACKAGE

In 2009, I was introduced through a mutual friend to Ronii Bartles. Ronii is a West Virginia woman living in Charleston, South Carolina and loving every minute of it. She's a marketer with a keen eye for design. Completely detail-oriented, Ronii flawlessly executes every marketing project she takes on. She communicates well, is a people person, and will unabashedly rave about her love of wine. Ronii is an independent, focused, and driven entrepreneur who knows how to kick butt and take names. As a blogger, she enjoys creating content for her clients and for herself. She revels in storytelling and dropping in one-liners, which is why I love reading her marketing blogs.

Without fail she creates fantastic content, enjoyed by many people including me. By doing so, I really started to understand Ronii—what she was like 10 years ago and who she is now. I learned what she enjoyed doing—her work, her hobbies, and the other things that mattered to her. All these lessons about her are sprinkled throughout her content. She always finds a way to put herself into her stories. Sometimes she pours herself into her blogs. At other times she drizzles her blogs with little bits of gold, nuggets of detail and additional information about her and her life.

One day I was reading her latest blog in my office and a lightbulb went off. It illuminated her article like a lamp post on a very dark country road. The specific blog content escapes me, but I'll never forget one morsel she sprinkled into that article.

Buried in her blog was a single line that professed her love of chocolate-covered bacon. What? Yes! Bacon and chocolate all mixed into one. I immediately put an employee on the task of hunting down chocolate-covered bacon. It took a while, but finally, after about an hour, we found the perfect gift and shipped it to Ronii in South Carolina.

Within hours after it arrived, her social media pages up lit up like a Christmas tree, and it was June, not December! Ronii posted pictures, stories, and details about the chocolate-covered bacon, and my web agency, inConcert Web Solutions. Not exactly what I was expecting, but, hey, I'll take it!

Looking back, I wonder why I didn't expect her to enthusiastically post on social media. After all, she was a skilled marketer. I should have known she would immediately share the story online.

In the weeks that followed I couldn't stop thinking about the string of actions that resulted in the social media posts. Those days of thinking were the seeds that grew into *CarePackage*. It took me years to nail down the framework and get the business results.

The reality is you don't have to be Ronii. You don't have to be a skilled marketer to share positive things on social media. People are sharing the love on social media these days and you should too because you'll find that it creates more word of mouth referrals. That's just one of many things you can do to create relationships that build deeper connections and tighter bonds with your contacts.

Ronii became a continued source of referrals for my website agency for many years. She still refers business to inConcert even after I sold it in 2018. Why does she refer?

Because of chocolate-covered bacon? Probably not. But, frankly, it might be part of it.

The Premise

It's well known that people do business with those they know, like, and trust. But I actually think it's more than that. I believe that people want to do business with those they not only know, like, and trust, but also that they *care* about. Ronii had a vested interest in referring us. She needed a trusted source that would do what they said, on time and on budget. We did that consistently. But she also needed someone who would call her back, which seems to be a widespread problem in the website world. It wasn't a problem for us, though, so we became a reliable, responsive company people could reach. In fact, 65% of our new clients told us that they couldn't get in touch with their current provider.

Throughout the 16 years that I owned the web agency, I always looked for the best ways to do things. My focus was on optimization and automation. Yet I continued to return to the one thing that really matters—one-to-one communication between trusted contacts. Our website agency constantly found ways to ensure that we remained top of mind with our contacts.

When I present to a group of business owners about marketing and advertising, I ask, "With a show of hands, how many of you feel that word of mouth is the number one way you get new business?" Overwhelmingly the answer is greater than 90 percent. Then I ask, "How many of you have a process to increase your word of mouth referrals that does not include asking, because that never works?" The results are disheartening. It was always less than 10 percent.

If we know and believe that we get the majority of our clients from word of mouth referrals, then why are we not working every day to increase our number of referrals? I get it, life gets in the way, and we find new shiny objects. That happened to me as well. But the final four years that I owned my agency, nearly 75 percent of all new clients were referred by our partners—people who continuously sent us referrals. The remaining 25 percent was divided between clients and other sources. That 25 percent was divided up into two categories—clients (20 percent) and other (5 percent). Other was comprised of sources that we did not know and Google search results. We didn't get any new website clients from advertising!

We tracked these numbers diligently. Not only did we ask the clients when we were onboarding them how they found us, but we noted it in our CRM (Customer Relationship Management) Software and in their file. We were obsessed with understanding this matrix. And the reason you should be obsessed with this as well is that it's a repeatable system of communication that results in more word of mouth referrals. After all, you need to know with whom to communicate with in order to increase your referral numbers.

Rule Number One: Stay in Touch

Regardless of how much you think you might be bothering someone, if you fail to stay in touch, you will fail to get referrals. On the contrary, though, if you find unique ways to reach out to your contacts, you will get more referrals. It's that simple. The reason businesses advertise and do marketing is that they want to be top of mind when someone is looking for their service. I would argue that constantly reaching out makes you top of mind and positions you to receive more referrals.

Personal CarePackage

To cut through the noise of marketing and advertising that bombards your contacts every day, you must find some very clever ways to reach them. Developing your personal care package is the key. This is a series of things you do to ensure that you remain on the top of your contact's mind. It will be different for each contact, but not drastically different. For example, if you decide to send something to a contact, it might be chocolate-covered bacon, or perhaps it will be a custom bag of trail mix, created specifically for your contact. You'll need to know what your contact likes to ensure you deliver the item that's perfect for them.

I call this process your personal *CarePackage*. Perhaps you've been lucky enough to receive a care package from someone in your life. Care packages are created with the recipient in mind. That's the goal of this process. It's about the recipient, and not about you.

THE FOUR PILLARS OF CAREPACKAGE

Before I dig deep into the four pillars, it's important to know that you are sending care packages because you care about your contact. If you are doing this specifically to get a referral, it won't work, and you'll regret it in the long run. If you are not genuine in your care for them, your contacts will see right through it.

In the book, *Never Lose a Customer Again*, my friend and author Joey Coleman wrote, "The best presents are meaningful and personalized. They exhibit a level of care and consideration commensurate with the relationship." To me, presents aren't just physical gifts. They are gifts of time as well. They are personal touch phone calls and personal emails. Gifts of your time and effort, personalized toward your contact. Word of mouth referrals are byproducts of caring for others. Your care for them will result in care for you and for your business.

Pillar 1 – Over-delivery

By nature, the potential for over-delivery exists where there is a transaction of some sort. Transactions generally involve money; however, they don't have to, especially if you are volunteering. It's absolutely imperative for you to find ways to ensure that you are not just meeting your clients expectations but you are exceeding them. When you over-deliver, you do so because you care about your client, and the results they are getting from you or your service. Because you care, and because the over-delivery is clear to your contact, they will lean more toward referring you to others they know.

I am often asked the same question as it pertains to over-delivery. "Should you under-promise and over-deliver?" Simply put—no. When you under-promise, you are doing so just for the sole purpose of over-delivering, and that is dishonest.

Pillar 2 - Listening

The standard definition of listening focuses on the auditory aspect—using your ears to listen. However, the Merriam-Webster dictionary defines listening in three ways:

- "to pay attention to sound"
- "to hear something with thoughtful attention: give consideration"
- "to be alert to catch an expected sound"

While all these definitions reference sound or hearing, I would argue that you can also listen with your eyes. What if we removed or replaced the references to sound and hearing in the Merriam-Webster definitions with visual terms? Here's what they would look like:

- "to pay attention to ~~sound~~"
- "to ~~hear~~ *see* something with thoughtful attention: give consideration"
- "to be alert to catch ~~an~~ "something" expected ~~sound~~"

Imagine for a moment how the world would look if you listened to or observed your contacts knowing that they were going to share information about themselves that would be incredibly useful to you in future conversations.

Pillar 3 - Surprise

The act of surprising someone with your actions is powerful. Comedians routinely use surprise in their jokes. They set you up with context, then they throw out the punchline which is rarely something you expected. One reason comedians get laughs is that their punchlines are unexpected.

Consider this: you order something on Amazon and it arrives in two days with Prime shipping. You aren't likely to have butterflies in your stomach when you see the package at your front door. But then the next day an unexpected package arrives. You immediately glance at the return address to figure out who sent the package. Your pulse quickens. *Who sent this? What could possibly be in this box?* The sender has already made an amazing impression and you haven't even opened the package. The surprise effect is such a powerful way to connect with someone, regardless of who they are.

Pillar 4 – Non-self-serving Acts

Your actions should be of service to your contact, and not you. For example, let's say you love chocolate, however, your contact is allergic to it. Imagine the effect if you sent your contact a package of chocolate. The experience would start with eager anticipation. *Who sent me a package? What could it possibly be?* And then your contact would open it only to discover it's chocolate and they cannot partake. The lasting impression would be negative despite your good intentions.

A self-serving act I see all the time is when people send thank you cards and include a business card. When you send a thank you card, the card must be all about the contact. However, the minute you include a business card, you've turned that experience into something about you. It's no longer a gift of time, effort, or a card; it's simply a method of sending your business card through the mail, and as such, it is self-serving.

When you remove yourself and your marketing materials from the mix, you create a non-self-serving act, which is a key component to your personal *CarePackage*!

Combining Pillars

These pillars aren't meant to be plucked from the book and executed alone. They are often combined, to create very meaningful experiences and interactions with your contact. Let's look at the chocolate-covered bacon with Ronii again. In that case, I listened with my eyes, I heard what she wrote, and then I surprised her. All of which was not self-serving. I didn't ask for anything in return, and I didn't post anything on social media indicating that I sent the gift. In this case, I combined three of the four pillars to make this happen.

Quite often I find that clients I work with aren't seeking out the pillar to work within or to use. Instead, they take action with their contact, then they generally reflect on that action and the pillar(s) it fit into. Reflecting after you take action is a great way to continue to analyze how you are effectively caring for your contacts.

The tactics that I have used over the years are featured in this book. My hope is that you'll see this book as a resource to turn to when you want to connect deeper with your contacts.

BIRTHDAYS BEYOND FACEBOOK: BIRTHDAY CARD REVIVAL

Let's face it. No matter how many birthdays you've celebrated, each one is special. And when people remember your birthday, you never forget. With the advent of Facebook, celebrating birthdays is as simple as a few clicks—a quick birthday wish with a little flair, perhaps a cake or balloon icons. Some people might even post a celebratory image. We get a recognition rush when we see 200 birthday messages on our Facebook wall. And, while the rush gives us a boost, it is fleeting. We know that 200 people took the path of least resistance.

Instead, let's find a more genuine way to connect with our contacts around birthdays. Because everything old is new again, let's bring back a long-cherished tradition that shows you truly value your relationships. Keep a stack of funny, thoughtful, and clever birthday cards on your desk with stamped envelopes. Then all you have to do is select the perfect one for your contact, address it, write happy birthday with a short personal note, and pop it in the mail. The note is the key here. Make it short, but make it personal and relevant to previous conversations. It's a super easy way to show you are thinking of your contact, and it cuts through the Facebook noise. Who doesn't love to receive a personal card amidst junk mail and bills? Your contact will never forget your special touch.

TIP...

IF YOU DON'T KNOW YOUR CONTACT'S BIRTHDAY, IT'S EASY TO FIGURE OUT WITH A LITTLE FACEBOOK SLEUTHING. MANY FOLKS WILL LIST THEIR BIRTHDAY WITHOUT THE YEAR, BUT FORTUNATELY THAT'S NOT REQUIRED WHEN SENDING A THOUGHTFUL BIRTHDAY MESSAGE.

JAVA JUMPSTART

What's better than taking a coffee break in the middle of a hectic, deadline-driven day with back-to-back meetings? A freshly-brewed piping-hot cup of coffee delivered directly to you when you least expect it. There's no doubt that a surprise java jumpstart will make your contact's day. When you drop off the cup of joe, quickly say hello and add that you thought they'd appreciate a coffee break. When doing this, it's important to respect their time.

If you don't know how your contact takes their coffee, opt for black with cream and sugar on the side. Leave the doctoring up to them. When you drop by with your special delivery, ask them how they take their coffee and make a note of it in the notes section of their contact record on your phone. Next time, you'll bring them their favorite caffè latte.

TIP...

DON'T OVERSTAY YOUR WELCOME. UNLESS YOUR CONTACT INVITES YOU TO STAY, SPEND NO MORE THAN FIVE MINUTES AT THEIR OFFICE. MAKE IT SHORT AND SWEET.   YOU WANT THEM TO REMEMBER THE COFFEE SURPRISE, NOT YOUR INTERRUPTION OF THEIR PRESSING PRIORITIES.

THANK YOU FOR YOUR BUSINESS

Always keep a package of thank you cards in your desk. You never know when you're going to need one. Giving thanks is one of the simplest ways to let your contacts know you appreciate them. When a contact decides to do business with you, take some time to send them a thank you note.

So often in business, we get stuck chasing the new sale, but the minute we get it, we immediately move on to the next sale. Take a moment—a moment of gratitude, and thank your contact for giving you some business. We are often very thankful for the business—we just don't always express it in a way that our contact notices. After all, these folks are the reason you are still in business.

Here is an example of a thank you note I send:

> Hello Lisa,
>
> Thank you for having me speak at your conference. I truly appreciate it, and I'm grateful for the trust you've placed in me. The conference was full of energy and the audience was so receptive. It was such a great experience for me.
>
> I look forward to staying in touch. Please let me know if I can help you in any way.
>
> With gratitude,
>
> Matt

TIP...

TAKE FIVE OR TEN MINUTES TO DRAFT A GENERIC THANK YOU FOR YOUR BUSINESS NOTE THAT YOU CAN USE AS A TEMPLATE. THEN, WHEN IT'S TIME TO THANK A SPECIFIC CONTACT, CUSTOMIZE THE NOTE TO YOUR CONTACT. THE FINISHING TOUCHES ARE WHAT WILL MAKE YOUR CONTACT FEEL EXTRA SPECIAL.

SWAGALICIOUS

You might not know that "SWAG" is an acronym for Stuff We All Get. But the thing about swag is: we don't all have access to the same stuff. And you might just have some swag that your contacts would love. Easy access swag, stuff readily available at your office, is a no-brainer. Know your contacts' taste, select swag especially for them, package it up, and send it off. They'll be thrilled.

Go beyond easy access swag and you'll delight your contacts even more. For example, if you attend a trade show or an expo, and you know a contact of yours is crazy for highlighters, keep an eye out for exhibitors giving them away. Make the rounds and collect a bunch. Then put together a small package of highlighters from the trade show with a note to your contact. They'll be in highlighter heaven for years and will think of you fondly.

A friend of mine worked at a radio station, where she had access to top-notch swag. I had serious swag envy! She scored tickets to Six Flags, ski lift tickets, movie passes, concert tickets, festival passes, t-shirts from a variety of brands, and branded apparel from the radio station. Every time she got something, she would stop by a contact's office and gift them one of these fabulous giveaways. They loved it. Who wouldn't? Everyone loves receiving gifts even if it's swag. Bonus points if the swag you always give out is not branded with your company information.

TIP...

YOU CAN BECOME A SWAG-SCORING MACHINE. KEEP AN EYE OUT FOR COOL SWAG AT FESTIVALS, CONCERTS, RACES, ART SHOWS, AND SPORTING EVENTS. YOU NEVER KNOW WHEN YOU'LL FIND THE PERFECT GIFT FOR ONE OF YOUR CONTACTS AND MAKE THEIR DAY.

R.E.S.P.E.C.T.

Who doesn't love to receive positive feedback? As the old saying goes: people won't remember what you said, but they will remember how you made them feel. In our frenzied world, people sometimes forget to take the time to share their positive thoughts for their friends, family, and contacts. With a high-tech world, people often forgo high touch. You can use this to your advantage and really stand out from the crowd.

Take some time to identify your contacts' strengths and the traits, habits, and characteristics you truly respect them for. Then select the best way to communicate this respect to them. Tailor the approach to the person. You can share your feelings in person, over the phone, with a card, or via email. I'd recommend using email as your last option because it's less personal and may get lost in the barrage of emails in your contact's inbox.

Here are some examples of things to look for in your contacts that you might respect:

- Hustle and Drive
- Commitment
- Positive attitude
- Financial acumen
- Daily habits
- Morning routine
- Sense of calm
- Time management
- Leadership
- Articulate
- Thoughtfulness

TIP...

WHEN YOU SHARE WHAT YOU RESPECT ABOUT YOUR CONTACT, ADD A SPECIFIC EXAMPLE THAT ILLUSTRATES THE HABIT, TRAIT, OR QUALITY. THEN THEY'LL SEE THAT YOU'RE PAYING ATTENTION AND YOU TRULY MEAN WHAT YOU SAY.

#NEWSWORTHYSHARING

We live in an era of oversharing on social media—pics of foodie meals, photos of silly pet tricks, and selfies galore—the Eiffel Tower as a hat. Oui! Oui! And holding up the Leaning Tower of Pisa. Don't let it fall! *I share, therefore I am* is the dictum of our time. Let's face it: some things are more share-worthy than others—like your contacts' big news. Finally some news that should stop the presses.

Perhaps your contact is having a special holiday sale or a celebratory ribbon cutting. Maybe they're unveiling a brand new product or service, or they have just launched a dazzling new website. Share newsworthy updates about your contact's business on your social media accounts and tag them. By tagging your contact, you let them know that you have shared their news. Sharing their content demonstrates that you care about your contact and their business. After all, if they posted it, they want to get the word out. Put social media to good use and amplify **their** news! The more, the merrier!

TIP...

TAGGING IDENTIFIES SOMEONE ELSE IN A POST, PHOTO, OR STATUS UPDATE THAT YOU SHARE. IF YOU'RE USING FACEBOOK, INSTAGRAM, OR TWITTER USE @CONTACT'S NAME.

TAKE TIME TO GIVE THANKS

You can never thank people enough for their time, attention, or effort whether in person or using other means, like emails, texts or even cards. Pausing for a moment to express gratitude is well worth the effort.

To prepare for any occasion, buy a big package of thank you cards and keep them in your desk. After you meet with a contact, write out a thank you card. It doesn't have to be a long-winded letter - a short note will do the trick. Write, *thank you for taking the time to meet with me* and mention a couple of the things you spoke about. Make sure it's personalized. Avoid using generic content, as that will detract from the impact of the card. This isn't about expediting your time; it's about deepening and strengthening your relationships.

Here's an example of one I sent recently:

Hi John,

I appreciate you taking time out of your busy day to meet with me. I really enjoyed learning more about your passion and your business core values, and hearing the Taco Tuesday story! I hope your daughter's basketball team crushes their competition at the tournament this weekend. Looking forward to getting together again.

Be well,

Matt

TIP...

AFTER YOUR FACE-TO-FACE OR PHONE MEETING, SET ASIDE FIVE TO TEN MINUTES TO WRITE A THANK YOUR NOTE. THAT WAY YOUR CONVERSATION WILL BE FRESH AND YOU'LL BE BETTER ABLE TO ADD THE PERSONALIZED DETAILS THAT WILL HAVE A GREATER IMPACT.

BRIGHTEN SOMEONE'S DAY

There's almost nothing better than receiving a heartfelt compliment. It makes the person you are complimenting feel great and you can tell from their smile that you have brightened their day. What should you compliment your contacts on? Professional accomplishments, awards, key milestones, and anniversaries to name a few. Perhaps your contact scored a meeting that was important to them, made a big sale, launched a new product, landed a hard-won contract, or ran a successful event. Look at your contacts' social media feeds to discover what they are sharing and how they feel about their accomplishments. This may give you the information you need to pay your contact a compliment. And you will make their day.

TIP...

MAKE SURE YOU STICK TO BUSINESS-RELATED COMPLIMENTS. YOU DON'T WANT YOUR COMPLIMENTS TO MAKE YOUR CONTACTS FEEL UNCOMFORTABLE.

BE KNOWN AS A CONNECTOR

Each of us sits on a goldmine of potential connections. We all have networks that can be tapped to propel our contacts to the next level. What's missing is the method by which to link people up. Sure, we have LinkedIn, but those connections are algorithmic, lacking a personal touch. That's where you come into the picture.

You may know someone that one of your contacts wants to meet. Go ahead and make that introduction. The connection will be beneficial for your contact, the third party, and you. Being a connector helps build deep and fulfilling relationships. When people discover they can come to you to get connected to others and to find resources they need, you will be in high demand.

I recently received a text message from a friend named Keven, asking me if I knew someone who could equip and install video conferencing software for his company's conference room. Keven knew I was well-connected and would be able to get him what he needed. I reached out to my network and connected him with the perfect person. This happens to me a lot, because I make it clear to everyone that I have a strong, reliable network and proactively connect others. You'll be delighted to learn that building networks is a gift that keeps on giving.

TIP...

DON'T WAIT FOR A CONTACT TO COME TO YOU ASKING FOR A CONNECTION. BE PROACTIVE ABOUT MAKING INTRODUCTIONS AND CONNECTING OTHERS. YOU NEVER KNOW; THE NEXT CONNECTION COULD CHANGE SOMEONE'S LIFE AND YOUR CONTACT WILL BE FOREVER GRATEFUL.

KNOWLEDGE IS POWER

Many people believe that knowledge is power. And in the digital age, knowledge of tools and applications certainly gives people a leg up. Think about the tools, apps, and software in which you are proficient, and consider which ones might benefit your contacts. Although you may take your skills and know-how for granted, you never know when such shared knowledge might take a specific contact of yours to the next level. There's nothing better than helping a contact learn something you are already good at. Reach out to them to gauge their interest. If they are game, commit to training them and set up a time for doing so. The respect gained from your contact will be invaluable, and it will truly demonstrate that you care about them and their success.

TIP...

IF YOUR CONTACT LIVES IN A DIFFERENT CITY, OFFER TO TEACH THEM A TOOL BY CONDUCTING A VIRTUAL SESSION USING A COLLABORATIVE PROGRAM SUCH AS WEBEX, ZOOM, OR SKYPE. IT'S THE NEXT BEST THING TO BEING THERE.

MAKE A SPLASH WITH A PERSONALIZED GIFT

If you think about the most meaningful gifts you have received, it's likely the ones that took into account your personality, passions, and interests—that were customized to you. Personalized gifts have more intrinsic value than a generic gift. When you consider giving a gift to a contact, use your heart and mind to think of something that will be meaningful to **them**. Be intentional with your gift. But how can you gather the information you need to personalize a gift without giving away the surprise? Here's how I did it.

I was planning to attend an event and I really wanted to share with the host that the content he was putting out had helped me. I had read his book and listened to all of his podcasts, even ones where he was a guest. I wanted to say *thank you* in a memorable way.

I connected the dots based on what he had shared about his life. I knew he had a boat and friends enjoyed drinking wine (even though he doesn't allow Red Wine) on his boat. My idea was to send him a personalized gift using the name of his boat. But I didn't want to ask him directly because I wanted to surprise him. Through internet sleuthing, I discovered his boat's name and the logo. I ordered a wooden wine opener set with the name of his boat engraved on the corkscrew. And he absolutely loved it! It cost me less than $30 and it made quite a splash.

TIP...

FIND OUT WHAT MATTERS TO YOUR CONTACT THROUGH CONVERSATIONS, EMAILS, SOCIAL MEDIA POSTS, OR CONTENT THEY GENERATE, SUCH AS BLOG POSTS, PODCASTS OR VIDEOS.

BOOST YOUR CONTACTS' INDUSTRY KNOWLEDGE

Although your contacts know that learning about their industries will enhance their knowledge and ultimately make them better businesspeople, they rarely take time to do this. Why? Because they're too busy delivering their products and services to their customers. What's the solution? Do the research for them!

Sharing cutting-edge resources and articles with your contacts will keep you on the top of their mind. Plan to send an article to a different contact each week. Try to do this at a specific time each week. Don't spend more than 10 minutes researching articles to find the right one for that week's contact. Once you master this, add one or two additional contacts to double or triple your reach!

The key to this article and resource share is to include a simple note as part of your email that references why you thought the resource or article would be useful to them. Use your judgment as to the number of articles you send. Keep in mind that if you send too many as part of the same email, your contact may feel overwhelmed and it won't be effective. They'll simply glance over the email, never read the article and the resource share will be ineffective.

I have done this consistently over the years and I always get great feedback from my contacts. They clearly appreciated that I went above and beyond for them.

TIP...

SET UP A GOOGLE ALERT. ENTER KEYWORDS RELATED TO YOUR CONTACT'S INDUSTRY AND GOOGLE WILL DO THE REST. YOU WILL RECEIVE ARTICLES AND EVENT NOTIFICATIONS BY EMAIL RELATED TO THE KEYWORD YOU USED FOR THE ALERT. THEN GRAB THE ARTICLE LINK AND SEND IT TO YOUR CONTACT.

GENIE IN A BOTTLE

Who doesn't want a genie in a bottle who can answer all their questions and grant all their wishes? Guess what? You do have a genie at your fingertips that can immediately respond to all your inquiries. It's called Google. Unfortunately, it can't grant all of our wishes yet, but hopefully that's in the works! For those who gathered information the old school way—using libraries and encyclopedias—Google is nothing short of miraculous.

Google not only responds to searches about things like how to set up QuickBooks, how to create a viral video, and how to get more clients; it can also help you build relationships with your contacts. If you want your contact to know you're thinking about him or her, consider this idea. Google your contact's industry or something that's relevant to their business. Search for websites that will inspire your contact and ignite their passion and purpose. Identify sites with the potential to positively impact their product or service offerings and bottom line. Carefully vet the websites to determine the ones that would be the most valuable.

After identifying a handful of websites, include the links and a note in an email indicating the ways in which you think the websites will benefit your contact's business. Your contact will be wowed by your initiative and see that you go the extra mile. You will remain top of mind as a resource to tap when they need your products or services. In our frenzied world in which people are too busy for the special touches, a little legwork goes a long way.

TIP...

YOU HAVE A GENIE AT YOUR FINGERTIPS THAT CAN IMMEDIATELY RESPOND TO ALL YOUR INQUIRIES. USE THE GOOGLING GENIE TO WOW YOUR CONTACTS AND REMAIN ON THE TOP OF THEIR MIND.

DON'T WORRY.
CURIOSITY NEVER KILLED THE CAT

C ontrary to the popular saying, curiosity never killed the cat. And it won't kill you. In fact, quite the opposite, expressing curiosity about your contact's life will open doors you didn't even know existed.

Let's say you're meeting at your contact's office and as you stroll in, you notice photos of her family bungee jumping. It looks like they were in New Zealand or Australia. Why do you think this? She is posing with a kangaroo in the collage. You inquire about the photo collage and your contact describes a trip of a lifetime that was always on her bucket list. True, her family had a harrowing incident with a crocodile, but they survived to tell the tale. She calls it "The Croc Almost Ate My Husband." You're both in stitches about it.

On the opposite wall hangs abstract artwork that you admire and you ask about the artist. She pauses and proudly says it's hers. You say you thought it was created by someone famous and she's clearly flattered by your praise.

By taking a few minutes to notice her world and to ask about her story, you've made a priceless connection with your contact. You didn't take notice to sell something, or even to ask for something in a selfish way. You took notice to build respect and deepen your relationship with your contact. People love to talk about themselves, their hobbies, and their families. When they have the chance, they will remember you as someone who is genuine—a person they can trust with their business.

TIP...

EXPRESSING CURIOSITY ABOUT YOUR CONTACT'S LIFE WILL OPEN DOORS YOU DIDN'T EVEN KNOW EXISTED. USING THE RULE OF THREE, TRY TO ASK THREE RELEVANT AND RELATED QUESTIONS. THIS ALLOWS YOU DIG DEEPER INTO THE TOPIC.

READ ALL ABOUT IT!

If your contact is in the newspaper or is featured in a magazine, grab the link of the article and send it to a local awards company to have a plaque made. It's not every day that people are featured in the news, and this shows that you are paying attention and care about your contact.

Without fail when I have done this for others, it has resulted in a hug. Although that is certainly not the goal, people are amazed that you have taken the time to create a memento for them. The perceived value of this gift far exceeds the actual cost.

I did this once for Jack, a fairly new employee at an IT company. He shared an article on Facebook from the local business journal discussing an award that his company had just received. I don't know the full backstory, but Jack was featured in the photo, posing in front of the company sign, and not the owner. I was intrigued by this and wanted to make sure Jack had a permanent copy of the article. So, I captured the moment by having a plaque made. And, in case you're wondering... Jack gave me a hug!

TIP...

WHEN YOU PLACE YOUR ORDER, CUSTOMIZE THE PLAQUE TO THE PERSON. IF YOUR CONTACT IS TRADITIONAL, OPT FOR A CLASSIC WOODEN PLAQUE. IF YOUR CONTACT IS MORE FASHION-FORWARD, OPT FOR A MORE CONTEMPORARY STYLE.

TAP YOUR CONTACTS' EXPERTISE

Helping others improve personally and professionally is part of what makes the world go round. Sharing insights with others based on our experience helps us grow. People love to share their expertise to help others pursue their dreams. In the spirit of this goodwill, consider asking your contacts for business advice. I recommend sticking to business topics, but it depends on your relationship. Only you know if it's right to broach personal topics.

Seeking advice results in building a greater level of trust with your contacts. If you are a business owner, reaching out to a fellow business owner for advice is not only a great business growth and management strategy—hence masterminds—but it also shows your contacts that you respect their business acumen. They will likely be honored to share their expertise with you.

TIP...

MASTERMINDS ARE GROUPS OF LIKE-MINDED COLLEAGUES WHO MEET TO SHARE AND BRAINSTORM SOLUTIONS TO CHALLENGES AND TO HELP EACH OTHER GROW PERSONALLY AND PROFESSIONALLY. CONSIDER SEEKING OUT OR CREATING YOUR OWN MASTERMIND, SURROUNDING YOURSELF WITH PEOPLE WHOM YOU TRUST, AND TO WHOM YOU CAN TURN TO ON SHORT NOTICE.

IS ANYBODY LISTENING?

Have you noticed that we live in a noisy age, one in which everyone is competing for airtime? Whether it's a meeting, an after-work get-together, or colleagues sharing ideas informally; it seems that people have mastered the art of the monologue, but have lost touch with the art of communication. With so many people talking, is anybody really listening?

Think back to a time when someone remembered something significant you shared and brought it up again at a later time. Perhaps it was something positive like a promotion or an event you were stressed about, like a presentation to the board of directors of your company. How did it make you feel? You probably felt like your colleague cared enough to remember something you had shared with them. That colleague likely has a special place in your heart.

Communication is a two-way street, and, if no one is listening, are people really communicating? The ability to listen—not just hear—is a cultivated skill and an increasingly rare one. Listening is a key component in your personal care package.

Your contact might have mentioned they had a big meeting coming up or maybe they shared that their child's baseball team made it to the finals. Carve a little time out of your day to follow up with your contact and ask about the meeting or the game. Not only will your contact be delighted to share the outcome; they will be amazed that you remembered and cared enough to reach out. Simple touches like this are often lost in the digital age, which is exactly why it makes them more memorable.

TIP...

IF YOUR MEMORY ISN'T PARTICULARLY GOOD, JOT DOWN SOMETHING YOUR CONTACT SHARED AND MAKE A NOTE TO ASK THEM ABOUT IT LATER. THERE'S NO SHAME IN HAVING LITTLE REMINDERS THAT KEEP YOU CONNECTED TO YOUR CONTACTS.

A LITTLE HELP GOES A LONG WAY

When was the last time someone offered to help you with no strings attached? If you're like most of us, offers of help—even from friends and family—are probably few and far between. It's not that people don't care; it's just that most of us are too busy juggling all our responsibilities. If we were to add one more ball to the juggling act, they might all come tumbling down!

Even though you're, no doubt, crunched for time, I recommend checking in with your contacts on a regular basis and asking how you can help. Before you panic and think: *Are you kidding me? I don't have time*, hear me out. I'm not saying you should offer to help your contact with major projects like moving. I'm simply saying that reaching out and asking, "What can I do to help you?" is a great way to start your check-in conversations. You're simply offering up your time to help a contact. This offer means a lot, even if they don't take you up on it. The fact that you genuinely offered to help goes a long way.

TIP...

REMEMBER TO BE AS AUTHENTIC AS POSSIBLE. YOU DON'T WANT TO SOUND TOO "SALESY." OTHERWISE YOU WILL REEK OF ONE WITH STRINGS ATTACHED. SIMPLY APPROACH THIS CONVERSATION WITH A WILLINGNESS TO HELP.

LIGHTS, CAMERA, ACTION!

Have you ever wanted to produce, direct, and act in your own video? Now you can with Facebook Live. With so much competition for eyeballs on phones, tablets, and laptops, the challenge is to create something that really stands out. Videos definitely get more views and likes than still graphics or text.

Next time you are with a contact, create a quick Facebook Live video on your Facebook page. You can set up the video as a business discussion featuring your contact's business. This is free exposure for your contact. Even if your audience isn't their ideal audience, they will still value your intent to share their content with your audience.

What is a Facebook Live video, exactly? A live video is a real-time video post on Facebook. During your broadcast, you'll see the number of live viewers and a real-time stream of comments. When the broadcast ends, it will stay on your page's timeline.

TIP...

MAKE THE LIVE VIDEO ABOUT THEM!

1. HAVE A GOAL. KNOW WHAT YOU WANT TO COVER DURING THE LIVE VIDEO.

2. BECOME THE INTERVIEWER. ASK QUESTIONS ABOUT YOUR GUEST, THEIR BUSINESS, AND WHAT THEIR INDUSTRY IS LIKE.

3. LISTEN INTENTLY TO THEIR ANSWERS AND ASK RELEVANT FOLLOW-UP QUESTIONS.

A VIDEO CO-STAR IS BORN

Videos on social media have exploded in popularity in recent years. They often attract more attention than photos or images, and are more likely to be retweeted on Twitter. It's time to join the video revolution if you haven't already.

Ask a contact if they would like to be in a business-related video with you that you will post to Facebook, Instagram, Twitter, or YouTube. When you include your contacts, you share the spotlight with them. Although most people will be honored by your invite, some might resist the idea, because they are camera-shy. No problem! Your invitation simply shows you are thinking about them.

If your contact is game, they will probably ask questions about the content and purpose of the video, and why you invited them. It's important to think about these questions before you invite your co-star. Establish your purpose beforehand so you are prepared. Most clients I work with use videos like this to showcase their contacts' business, in bite-sized interviews, no longer than three minutes. Once the business is out of the way, have fun shooting it. The livelier it is, the more attention you will attract. Who knows - maybe it will go viral!

TIP...

ONCE YOU SHOOT THE VIDEO, UPLOAD IT TO SOCIAL MEDIA, TAGGING ALL THE PEOPLE IN THE VIDEO AND MAYBE SOME YOU THINK WOULD BE INTERESTED IN VIEWING THE VIDEO. CONSIDER ADDING A CALL TO ACTION IN YOUR POST, SUCH AS CONTACT INFORMATION FOR YOUR CLIENT OR CONTACT AND A PLUG FOR THEIR PRODUCTS OR SERVICES. THIS FUN VIDEO COULD BE AN EXCELLENT PROMOTIONAL OPPORTUNITY FOR YOU AND YOUR CONTACT.

CUTTING THROUGH THE NOISE

When did we all become so busy that it's dizzying? Our email inboxes overflow with questions, requests, and tasks that must be completed. The deadline, no matter what the task, is ASAP, which really means yesterday. Some of us have even developed an allergy to our email inboxes. So, what's the best way to cut through the noise of email?

Since most of us are glued to our smart phones, texting is an excellent way to cut through the noise. The only tricky part is determining those that text versus those that don't among your contacts. Some will be open to texting; others not so much. Once you figure out which contacts are receptive, consider using this means of communication occasionally. In my experience, texting gets a much quicker response even if it's just an acknowledgment, a thumbs up, or a smiling emoji. Keep in mind that texting often lacks a personal touch, so don't overuse it.

Here are some examples of texts to send your contact:

- Congratulations on closing the deal!
- How did your presentation go today?
- Just checking in to see how your project is going.
- Did you ever get in touch with the lead we discussed?
- Just wanted to say hi!

TIP...

FOLLOW YOUR CONTACTS ON SOCIAL MEDIA, AND WHEN THEY SHARE GOOD NEWS OR A NOTEWORTHY STATUS UPDATE, IT'S A PERFECT TIME TO FOLLOW UP WITH A TEXT.

WHAT'S FOR LUNCH?

Everyone loves a free lunch but, as the saying goes, there's no such thing. You can change this misconception by treating your contacts to lunch once a month—no strings attached. If there are no strings attached, then what's the agenda, what's on the menu so to speak, or as I like to say… "What's for lunch?" Answer: Leveraging your network to enable your contacts to make connections and assist each other with business opportunities, issues, and challenges. In other words, helping your contacts grow their networks and businesses. It will be a popular entrée to serve. Bottom line, these lunches serve as an opportunity for you to learn much more about your contact and how they fit into your network!

You'll want to gradually build the lunches and expand beyond just you and one other contact. Pick two or three contacts that complement each other in business, or invite contacts that would like to meet each other. Caution: This is not easy and requires some finessing. I recommend starting with one contact, then during lunch, find out who they would like to meet. Next month, invite that person for lunch. And voila! Now you have two guests. Allow this to grow over time. When I say grow, what I mean is, you cap the lunch attendees at 4 people, but consider doing more than one of these lunches each month! Schedule this as a monthly event on your calendar, and be sure to schedule reminders to reach out to people to actually get them on the schedule.

TIP...

READ JAYSON GAIGNARD'S BOOK, *MASTERMIND DINNERS.* THIS IS A PLAYBOOK FOR THOSE WHO WANT TO CREATE AND CULTIVATE MEANINGFUL RELATIONSHIPS. THIS BOOK EXPLORES HOW TO HOST DINNERS THAT RESULT IN CONNECTIONS FOR OTHERS AND THAT ALLOW YOU TO LEVERAGE YOUR NETWORK TO SOLVE PROBLEMS FOR OTHERS. IT'S QUITE A PROCESS AND JASON HAS LAID IT OUT VERY WELL.

FROSTY FRIDAYS

There's nothing better than treating your taste buds to a Wendy's Frosty, especially on a hot day or even on a not-so-hot day. Let's face it, Frosties are so delicious, people enjoy them any time of year. Part milkshake, part ice cream, this treat is unrivaled. Wendy's has been famous for their Frosties for decades. And you can become famous by association. Quickly make a name for yourself in your local business community by treating your contacts to a Frosty on Fridays. Here's the reality, Frosty Fridays are a lot more fun and easier than Taco Tuesdays. Why? It's not that tacos aren't delicious; it's just that they have too many moving parts for easy delivery.

Frosty Friday is not just about the Frosty; it's about making your contacts feel appreciated. Buy a few Frosties every Friday and drop by your contact's office. They'll love a Wendy's tasty treat. As you move through your contacts list, word will spread and you'll start receiving requests like, "Hey, when are you stopping by for Frosty Friday?"

You'll give TGIF a whole new meaning. In fact, because of you, TGIF will become TGIFF—Thank God it's Frosty Friday (TGIFF)!

TIP...

TO KEEP THE FROSTIES SUPER CHILLED, REMEMBER TO KEEP A COOLER IN YOUR CAR. YOU'LL BE LIKE AN ICE CREAM TRUCK, ONLY BETTER. YOUR CONTACTS WILL LOVE THEIR FREE HAND-DELIVERED TREATS.

BIZ BLOGGING

If you have a blog, include a post inspired by a contact and make sure to mention them. Many of your contacts write blogs, articles, or long-form social media posts. Use that information to inspire your blog posts. Then be sure to include your contact in the article and link back to their website. You'll also want to share the article with them.

For years people have asked me where they might seek inspiration for blogs and articles. There are many options: books you have read, your client's success stories, conversations in the office, or even frequently asked questions you receive while conducting business. But your contacts are one of the best places to start!

Invite your contacts who blog or write articles to be guest bloggers. Your contacts will be honored that you asked and it will drive traffic to your site, and benefit both you and your guest bloggers. It's a win-win!

TIP...

WHEN YOU'VE WRITTEN A BLOG POST INSPIRED BY A CONTACT, MAKE SURE TO POST A LINK ON FACEBOOK, LINKEDIN, AND TWITTER SO YOU CAN MAXIMIZE EXPOSURE AND DRIVE TRAFFIC TO YOUR BLOG. YOU SHOULD ALSO SEND AN EMAIL TO YOUR MAILING LIST WITH AN INSPIRATIONAL EXCERPT AND A LINK.

A CURE FOR THE MONDAY BLUES

There's nothing worse than a bad case of the Monday blues. You drag yourself to work, shuffle toward your office, and wish you were still at the ballgame or backyard barbeque with your friends. In fact, that sinking feeling of Monday morning dread usually creeps in on Sunday night. It's not that we don't like our jobs; it's just that our weekends are so full of fun, friends, and freedom that it takes some adjusting to get back to the grind.

It doesn't have to be like this. You have the power to change that for your contacts. No, you can't take away the inevitability of Monday morning, but you can surprise them with a freshly brewed coffee delivery. Your contacts will be so delighted by the coffee surprise, they will be able to tackle all that awaits them. All thanks to your special touch.

What's the best way to do this? Hand deliver it yourself. This could be a challenge if your contact is not local to you. If this is the case, consider using GrubHub.com to get the coffee picked up, HOT and delivered to your contact! This is your prescription to cure a case of the Monday blues.

TIP...

THROW IN SOME MUFFINS, SCONES, OR CROISSANTS WITH THE COFFEE--JUST WHAT THE DOCTOR ORDERED. IF YOU INCLUDE A DOZEN DONUTS, THEY'LL LOVE YOU EVEN MORE, JUST DON'T TELL THE DOCTOR ABOUT THOSE, HE WON'T BE TOO PLEASED WITH YOU.

VIRTUAL COFFEE

W ant to make your contact's day? Send them a virtual coffee by emailing them an ecard to their favorite coffee shop. Do not simply default to Starbucks; not everyone is a fan. Find out through casual conversation where they like to have coffee, and then order the gift card online. The gift card delivery will differ depending on where the card is from.

Once you've given the gift of java, it's a perfect opportunity to follow up with your contact and schedule a virtual coffee with them. Get a date on the calendar to connect. Then start the conversation with: "How's your coffee?"

TIP...

SOME COMPANIES ALLOW YOU TO SEND GIFT CARDS VIA IMESSAGE. FOR EXAMPLE, STARBUCKS JUST REQUIRES YOU TO ENABLE MOBILE PAYMENTS WHICH WORKS IN CONJUNCTION WITH THE STARBUCKS APP. FOR OTHER COM-PANIES' STEP BY STEP INSTRUCTIONS, GO TO THEIR WEBSITES.

OF MICE AND MEN

As the popular saying goes: the best-laid plans of mice and men sometimes go awry. This is from a poem by the Scottish poet Robert Burns, about a mouse that carefully builds a winter nest in a wheat field, only for it to be destroyed by a farmer. As with the hard-working mouse, things in business and in life don't always go as planned.

If one of your contacts is going through a rough patch—low sales, loss of a client, or their top performer left the company for another job—help them through it. Be present and available to listen—really listen—and remind them it won't always be like this. Sometimes all people need is for someone to reflect what they're feeling and to have faith in them when their faith in themselves is less than present.

Life is filled with ups and downs—it's quite the rollercoaster ride—and you don't always know the kind of day your contact is having. However, if you find out they are having a down day, reach out to them. Go out of your way to show your care and concern. That will make all the difference in the world, and it could turn their day around.

TIP...

WHEN YOU DISCOVER YOUR CONTACT IS HAVING A ROUGH TIME, IT'S A GREAT TIME TO SEND A HANDWRITTEN NOTE. THERE'S NOTHING LIKE A HEARTFELT CARD TO CONVEY THAT YOU'RE THINKING ABOUT THEM.

BRAIN HACKING WITH BOOKS

There's no easier or cheaper way to become an expert on a topic than by picking up a book that's packed with wisdom, practical advice, and tips. Let's say your contact is struggling with some aspect of their business or is interested in a new line of business and needs an easily accessible solution. This is where business book recommendations come in handy. Don't just recommend a book; go one step further. Send your contact a book that will help them hone their products or services, and increase customer satisfaction and sales.

When speaking with contacts about their businesses, I'll mention books that have had a significant impact on my business life. I always have at least one copy of my favorite books ready to ship. If I see that a contact is interested, I'll personalize a note in the front of the book and send it off. Every time I send a book, I order another one from Amazon. The reason that this matters to your contact is due to the personalized note that you write in the book. To do that you need to ensure that the books are shipped to you first. Never order a book and ship it directly to your contact.

Some of my favorite business books include:

- *Never Eat Alone* by Keith Ferrazzi
- *E-Myth* by Michael Gerber
- *Profit First* by Mike Michalowicz
- *Never Lose A Customer Again* by Joey Coleman
- *Unthink* by Erik Wahl

TIP...

KEEP BOOKS IN YOUR AMAZON CART WHERE YOU CAN MONITOR PRICE CHANGES. IF THE PRICE DROPS, BUY SEVERAL COPIES OF YOUR FAVORITE BOOK AND STOCK UP!

HOPE YOU CAN COME!

If your company has a customer appreciation night, invite your contact. If it's appropriate, also invite their significant other. Including your contact in your events, deepens your relationships. The effort to invite them won't go unnoticed, even if they cannot attend.

One summer I was invited to a customer appreciation night by the bank where I had my business account. The event was held at a modern art museum and included a band, an open bar, and a dinner with a seafood buffet. The event was absolutely amazing.

I had always been happy with my business bank and wouldn't have had a problem referring them, but the truth is I didn't really think about them much. If someone asked me who I used for business banking I would cite my bank's name, but if someone was considering taking out a loan or opening a business, I often didn't think to recommend my bank. The night of the event, I truly felt like a valued customer. Because of that, my bank made it to the top of my mind. When you invite your contacts to your special event, you will make a lasting impression.

TIP...

PAY SPECIAL ATTENTION TO WHICH CONTACTS YOU INVITE. IF YOU INVITE TOO MANY, YOUR TIME WILL BE DIVIDED AMONGST ALL OF THEM AND AS SUCH YOUR CONVERSATIONS WILL BE DILUTED AND REMAIN AT THE SURFACE LEVEL. LESS IS MORE IN THIS CASE. I KNOW THIS GOES AGAINST THE GRAIN OF TRYING TO FILL A ROOM, BUT THAT GOAL IS DIFFERENT FROM THE GOAL OF INVITING A CONTACT TO DEEPEN YOUR RELATIONSHIP.

PLAY MATCHMAKER

One way you can make a splash is by playing matchmaker for your contacts. Tap into your extensive network of contacts to make meaningful connections that will enhance your contacts' businesses.

What's the best approach for doing this? Take time to ask your contacts about their ideal referrals. Identify your contacts' goals for their business and seek to understand how they define a good referral—someone who can help them in their business. Dig deeply into this.

I find that some contacts aren't clear about who is ideal for them. For example, a banker might say, anyone who runs a business; however, when you dig deeper, that isn't the case. While it's true that a banker can work with someone in another part of the country, it's not ideal for the banker or the customer. So, if you were helping the banker network with others, you would focus on contacts in the banker's local area.

Pay close attention to what your contact says about their ideal referral, and then ask follow-up questions, trying to identify exactly who would be a good contact for them. Once you do, identify people in your network and make an introduction—either virtually or in person.

TIP...

ESTABLISH A BASIC LIST OF FIVE TO TEN QUESTIONS THAT YOU CAN ASK YOUR CONTACT TO DIG DEEPER INTO HOW THEY DEFINE THEIR IDEAL CLIENT. YOU MAY NOT USE ALL OF THESE EACH TIME, BUT YOU CAN START THE CONVERSATION AND DELVE INTO THESE QUESTIONS WHEN NEEDED.

GIVING BACK

Caring comes in many forms and taking time to give back to causes that are important to your contacts will show them that you truly care. Does your contact support a specific charity or organization that you would? If they do, provide an item for a fundraiser, make a donation to their favorite organization, volunteer with your contact, or get the word out for a charity event they are organizing.

When it comes to giving back, it's important to give because you want to, and not because your contact gives to that charity. This is not about obligatory giving. If you are planning to give to your contacts' charities, determine if they align with your beliefs. If so, then give. If not, don't! You should give because you want to, not just because your contact does so.

TIP...

THERE'S A NEW TREND IN WHICH PEOPLE CELEBRATE THEIR BIRTHDAYS BY FUNDRAISING FOR THEIR FAVORITE CAUSE OR CHARITY ON FACEBOOK. CONSIDER CONTRIBUTING TO YOUR CONTACTS' SELECTED CAUSES FOR THEIR BIRTHDAYS. IT'S QUICK, EASY, AND IT WILL MAKE AN IMPRESSION.

TRICKS OF THE TRADE

You typically know more about your products or services than your contacts do. Share a tip or trick that will make their life easier, regardless of whether they are using your products or services. For example, when I owned my website agency, getting content from clients was a huge challenge. We found that very few people were aware of transcription services that existed and all the different options that were available. These services allow for people to record audio and have it transcribed into the written word. Creating content was stressful for clients and these services made creating content less stressful, so we shared them with both clients and contacts. Sharing these ideas, suggestions and tips with your contacts can assist them in improving and streamlining their business processes and lives. They will be grateful for your expertise and your generosity in sharing what you know.

TIP...

BE SURE TO TRACK IN YOUR CRM OR A SPREADSHEET WHAT YOU ARE SENDING TO YOUR CONTACTS SO THAT YOU DON'T SEND THEM DUPLICATE TIPS OR SUGGESTIONS.

WHAT'S IN A NAME?

What's in a name? Well, everything. Dale Carnegie said, "A person's name is to him or her the sweetest and most important sound in any language."

Consider this: how does it feel when someone gets your name wrong? It comes across as if that person doesn't care enough to get it right. How about when someone surprises you by knowing your name when you don't even know theirs? You're delighted and a little embarrassed that you couldn't return the favor.

When interacting with a contact, make sure to use their name. When should you do this? Several times during each interaction. Let's say your contact's name is Connie. When greeting her, smile, shake her hand, and say, "Nice to see you again, Connie." When leaving, say, "Thank you for meeting with me today, Connie. I really appreciate it." Begin every email with, *Hi Connie*, and end with, *thank you, Connie.*

Now, make sure you don't overdo this. If you overuse your contact's name, as in inserting it in every other sentence, it can sound insincere. You don't want to come across like the bad stereotype of a used car salesperson. So, if this is new for you, start slowly and use your contact's name a few times during your exchange. Working a contact's name into a conversation may seem awkward at first, but you will adjust and see the benefits of the relationship grow.

When communicating by email, spend a little extra time ensuring that you spell your contact's name correctly. It will be well worth it. You can usually find their name in their email address or signature.

TIP...

IF YOU ARE UNSURE HOW TO PRONOUNCE A CONTACT'S NAME, THERE IS NO SHAME IN ASKING THEM HOW TO PRONOUNCE IT. IT IS BETTER TO ASK THAN TO MISPRONOUNCE OR AVOID USING IT.

PAUSE AND LISTEN

Imagine this: your contact calls you and they are really hyped up, but you are completely swamped. Your contact is talking a mile a minute about an aerospace stock that they invested in years ago and they are finally seeing a return. They are delving into specific details of the aerospace industry, as well as the history.

Is this something that you want to listen to right now? No! Is this something you are interested in? No! Are you going to give your contact your undivided attention? Yes! Why? Because you care about your contact and you know that listening is one of the key components of your personal care package. As you turn your attention to the conversation, you may soon develop an interest in aerospace, at least as it pertains to this conversation. Your contact will appreciate your undivided attention. And you never know—you could decide to invest in the aerospace stock and it could become your best investment ever!

TIP...

MOST OF US THINK WE'RE SKILLED AT MULTITASKING, BUT THE TRUTH IS: NONE OF US ARE. SO WHEN YOUR CONTACT CALLS AND TALKS ABOUT A SUBJECT THAT'S NOT PARTICULARLY INTERESTING TO YOU, TURN AWAY FROM YOUR DIGITAL DEVICES AND TRULY LISTEN. IF YOU'RE LOOKING AT YOUR EMAILS OR TEXT MESSAGES, YOU WON'T BE FULLY PRESENT AND IT WILL BE A MISSED OPPORTUNITY TO CONNECT WITH YOUR CONTACT.

FIVE STAR REVIEW

With social media reigning supreme in most industries, few things are more valuable for driving sales than rave reviews. And, on the contrary, a few scathing reviews can destroy a business. Glowing reviews are like gold in this era of social media domination and can really solidify trust for those looking for new services.

Consider taking 10 minutes out of your day to write a review for your contact on social media. There are lots of ways to review contacts and their businesses. A simple shout-out while tagging your contact on Facebook, Instagram, or Twitter will let your friends and followers know that your contact's business is trustworthy. For increased impact consider a formal review on a notable review site. You'll have to identify the site that reviews your contact's industry. For example, if your contact is in the travel industry, use websites like TripAdvisor or Yelp. Or if they are in the restaurant business, Open Table, Zagat, or Zomato are popular sites.

Becoming a raving fan is about sharing your experience as a customer, partner, or colleague. If you've never had a transaction then you can talk about the merits of your contact's integrity as a businessperson.

TIP...

TO WRITE A REVIEW, TAKE A QUICK PEEK AT THE OTHER REVIEWS AND MAKE SURE YOURS DOESN'T SIMPLY MIMIC EXISTING REVIEWS. WRITE SOMETHING NEW THAT SHOWCASES YOUR CONTACT'S BUSINESS IN AN ATTENTION-GRABBING WAY. DRAFT A REVIEW, EDIT IT, AND THEN POST IT FOR THE WORLD TO SEE.

GAME TIME!

I magine receiving a call from a contact inviting you to see your favorite sports team play. How awesome would you feel? Even if you can't attend, knowing that someone is thinking about you would make you feel great.

Consider inviting your contacts to a game to get caught up in the thrill of victory and the agony of defeat. Sporting events are shared experiences that go deeper than most. When you attend a game with someone who shares the love of the game and the love of the team, the camaraderie is unparalleled.

In 2018, I took one of my contacts to the AFC Championship game in Foxboro, Massachusetts. The New England Patriots hosted the Jacksonville Jaguars. We had a great time connecting on a personal level, sharing the game together, and experiencing yet another amazing come-from-behind win by Tom Brady. I've had similar experiences at hockey, golf, basketball, and badminton. Okay, maybe not badminton. But every game experience has been memorable and helped to cement my relationships with my contacts.

TIP...

TRY TO STEER CLEAR OF BUSINESS TALK DURING GAME DAY. JUST BE THERE FOR THE GAME, TO CONNECT, BUILD A DEEPER RELATIONSHIP, AND TO HAVE FUN!

FORE!

Yes, we're talking golf here. And while it might sound like a cliché', golf will never go out of fashion when it comes to bringing people together and garnering good favor. True, you don't want to invite a contact on a golf outing if they don't play – no better way to embarrass someone or bore them silly – but for those of us who do play, it's a great way to create a relaxed atmosphere that may or may not lead to business-related conversation. Even if it doesn't, the goodwill you've established will come back to you in spades.

I am always receiving notifications about golf tournaments in my area, because I've made a point of joining organizations that use golf for fundraising purposes. I automatically sign up for a foursome and intentionally invite three of my best contacts, people whom I know like golf. The beauty of it is, something as simple as 18 holes of golf establishes deeper connections that are both professional and personal. A no-brainer.

The reason this works is that you've taken the time to reach out to people who know you and your business, but you've taken the business out of it. You're playing golf with people you like and you're footing the bill. People remember that. Don't think that won't come back to you when someone needs your services. If your contacts end up helping each other, even better.

TIP...

JOIN ORGANIZATIONS THAT ORGANIZE GOLF TOURNAMENTS FOR FUNDRAISING PURPOSES, SUCH AS MAKE-A-WISH, ROTARY INTERNATIONAL, YOUR INDUSTRY ASSOCIATION AND YOUR LOCAL CHAMBER OF COMMERCE.

RED CARPET EVENTS

Who doesn't love to celebrate someone on the red carpet? Perhaps your contact is being honored at an industry event, having an open house, or a ribbon-cutting ceremony. Or maybe your contact is giving a keynote speech or offering a workshop. Especially if your contact is local, make sure you are there. You don't have to attend every event, but you should attempt to get to a few of them. This will make a huge impact. Your contact will be thrilled you took the time to attend their event. In fact, they will never forget it. Making the effort to honor them will make a lasting impression. Not only that, you'll learn more about them, their industry, and it will deepen and strengthen your relationship.

Consider attending a contact's out-of-town event. If you are planning an upcoming business trip, do some research on your contacts' events, show up, and surprise them! They will be touched and delighted and you will have a contact for life.

TIP...

TO STAY ON TOP OF YOUR CONTACTS' SPECIAL EVENTS, RESEARCH THEIR UPCOMING EVENTS AND CREATE A CONTACT SPREADSHEET. ADD THE EVENT INFORMATION FROM THE SPREADSHEET TO YOUR CALENDAR.

THE GRAND TOUR

When you are at your contact's place of business, ask for a tour, especially if it is a factory or warehouse. It's very likely you will learn something new about your contact, as well as their business and industry. Your contact will be flattered by your interest in their business. If a tour isn't available at the time, but you are offered one in the future, don't hesitate to get it on the calendar.

Whenever I am offered a tour, I enthusiastically accept the invitation. It's such a great learning experience for me and it gives me plenty of opportunities to ask questions and engage with my contact, which creates more understanding. The insight gained allows me to more effectively help my contact in the future.

TIP...

THIS IS A GREAT OPPORTUNITY, IF PERMITTED, TO SHOOT VIDEOS FOR FUTURE SHARING ON SOCIAL MEDIA. MAKE SURE TO ASK YOUR CONTACT FOR PERMISSION, AS SOME FACILITIES MAY FORBID PHOTOGRAPHY OF ANY KIND DUE TO THE SENSITIVE NATURE OF THE BUSINESS OR INDUSTRY.

PICK UP THE TAB

Attending networking events is a very effective way to grow your contact base, meet great people, and establish deeper more meaningful connections. While it can be effective to pick up the drink tab for one or more contacts, it's far more effective to pick up the registration tab for your contact to attend the event .

When you decide to attend an event, reach out to a few contacts and invite them along. Attending networking events is far less daunting for some people when they know that there will be a friendly face in the crowd as well.

This can make the event far more effective for you and for them.

TIP...

WHEN ONE OF YOUR CONTACTS ACCEPTS YOUR INVITATION AND ATTENDS THE EVENT, MAKE A POINT TO INTRODUCE THEM TO OTHERS THAT YOU KNOW. ADDITIONALLY, AS YOU MEET NEW PEOPLE THROUGHOUT THE EVENT, CIRCLE BACK AND INTRODUCE YOUR CONTACT TO THEM AS WELL.

EXTEND AN OFFER

The second pillar of your personal care package is listening. If you hear that your contact is going on a trip, volunteer to drive them to the airport. You will save them money, have time to reconnect on a personal level, and they will be very grateful for your assistance.

You might see on Facebook that they are looking for a dog sitter for the weekend, and you like dogs. Call them and volunteer to dog sit.

Maybe your contact is looking for someone to mow their lawn. If you have a teenager, send them over.

There are so many ways you can extend an offer and lend a hand, it's up to your imagination and your ability to listen to what is going on around you with your contacts.

TIP...

WHEN OFFERING TO LEND A HAND, DON'T ACCEPT ANY MONEY IN EXCHANGE FOR YOUR TIME OR WORK. IF YOU SEND OVER YOUR CHILD TO MOW THEIR LAWN, DON'T LET THEM ACCEPT MONEY. INSTEAD YOU PAY THEM FOR THEIR TIME AND WORK.

GOING ONCE...
GOING TWICE...
GONE!

Many businesses participate in local charity auctions, and sometimes they are very involved. Consider this as a great avenue to help your contact. Businesses get involved in charity auctions in many different ways. Sometimes they are organizing the event, other times they volunteer to help during the event, and then of course there are companies that are donating an auction item. Regardless of their level of involvement, you can find ways to participate with them and help their auction be a sweet success.

Are there items or services that you can donate from your business that they could in turn auction off? If your business is not well suited for auction donations, buy an item from another contact and donate that item to the auction. You'll be helping two contacts in this situation.

TIP...

TO START THE AUCTION CONVERSATION, SIMPLY SHARE WITH YOUR CONTACT A STORY ABOUT A PREVIOUS AUCTION YOU PARTICIPATED IN, THEN ASK IF THEY HAVE EVER DONE SIMILAR EVENTS. YOU'LL FIND OUT REALLY QUICK IF THEY ARE INVOLVED WITH ANY CHARITY AUCTIONS!

GETTING STARTED

In my experience, after introducing the concept of caring to audiences and clients, they get excited and rush out and buy Thank You Cards in bulk! A word of caution. Slow and steady wins this race.

My suggestion is that you start with six contacts and get to know them better. Start working on growing deeper connections with them. Understand who they are, what their needs are and look to give them referrals. Focus on these six contacts for the first 90 days.

Each month thereafter, consider adding one additional contact each month until you reach 12. Once you have your core 12 contacts, continue building your relationships with them for at least one full year without adding others into the mix.

This doesn't mean you ignore others, but it does mean you keep your focus on the 12.

I also suggest that the 12 key contacts be people you already have a relationship with. Ideally, they are someone that has potential to refer business. This won't always be the case, and there are exceptions to every rule, but I have found this to be the most successful way to jumpstart a word of mouth referral system.

Let it be known that not everyone you want to establish a relationship is interested in that. I have worked to grow relationships with people only to realize over time that they just aren't a relationship person. At some point, you need to move on. I'm not saying you shouldn't care any longer, I'm just saying that you shouldn't put the same amount of effort into building a stronger relationship with that contact.

So how do you know? They simply don't respond. This isn't determined by whether or not they give you referrals. It's determined by the fact that they engage. They reply. They call you back. If they are not engaging with you at all over a long period of time, that's when you say to yourself "It's not me, it's you"

FINAL THOUGHT

Over the course of building your personal CarePackage, you will see contacts come and go. That is normal. Embrace the process. There will be change within your contacts and understand that these changes are for the better. You'll be learning how to interact with your contacts as you go along, and your skills will grow. You'll get better at connecting, and you will start to see relationships in ways that you may have never seen them before.

This process for me started many years ago. It was slow in the beginning. I didn't reach out as much. I didn't get out of my comfort zone and give more. But now, I give all the time. I find ways to overdeliver as much as I feasibly can, while at the same time really understanding who I am talking to by listening to them and researching what they are all about. Sometimes, I even surprise myself with surprises for others! But at the end of the day, this isn't about me, this is about my contacts. Everything I do is in service of them, and I ensure I am driven by the fourth pillar in my personal CarePackage, Non-Self-Serving acts.

Note:

Submit your CarePackage results to:

CaseStudies@Breakthrough-Champion.com

I want to hear how you have implemented your Personal CarePackage with others. Did you send an ice cream party to someone's office? Deliver coffee? What happened? What response did you get? I'm compiling stories of CarePackages for my next book and would love to hear your stories! Send them over!

Note:

Go to

www.Breakthrough-Champion.com/Book

to take the free caring assessment! Once you get your score, work on different areas and try to improve them. Your awareness of the concept alone will now help you increase your score.

Questions?

I'm here for you. Send your questions to

<u>MoreBook@Breakthrough-Champion.com</u>

I'm happy to answer any questions you may have around caring for and connecting with others.

Want To Help Spread Caring?

If you are moved by the message of caring and the impact it can have on others, and you want to make an impact on your organization, reach out.

Speaking@Breakthrough-Champion.com